PEAK PERFORMING GOVERNANCE TEAMS:

Creating an Effective Board/Superintendent Partnership

Tim Quinn, Ph.D.

**with
Michelle E. Keith**

*Quinn and Associates, Ltd.
Old Mission, Michigan*

Published by Quinn and Associates, Ltd., PO Box 157, Old Mission, MI 49673

Other titles from this author include:

> *In the Arena: Building the Skills for Peak Performance in Leading Schools and Systems*
> *The Superintendent Search Process: A Guide to Getting the Job and Getting Off to a Great Start*

These titles, and additional copies of this book, are available through major online bookstores.

All profits from the sale of this book are dedicated to the continuing development of high needs youth.

ISBN-10: 1456331760
ISBN-13: 978-1456331764

PEAK PERFORMING GOVERNANCE TEAMS:
Creating an Effective Board/Superintendent Partnership

Foreword

Anyone who is even a casual observer of the public school business has noted the relatively high turnover rate among superintendents. Depending on the state and its laws regarding superintendents and boards, and the size and demographics of the school district, the average tenure for a superintendent may be anywhere between three and six years. A recent American Association of School Administrators study reported that on average, across America, the typical job term expectancy for a suburban superintendent is estimated to be six years, and the tenure of an urban superintendent a little over three years.

Research has made it clear that this churn at the top of the organization does little to advance the success of school districts in preparing every student to be competitive in today's global market place.

The causes for this high turnover are many. *These are tough jobs*, performed in a very public arena. School districts customarily consume more public tax dollars than any other local governmental entity, and thus operate under the magnifying glass of significant public and media scrutiny. They often employ more people than any other organization in their community. Districts also operate within the context of volumes of federal and state statutes, administrative rules, and existing community norms. Add to that equation the fact that the primary business of schools is to develop a community's most precious asset—its children. Then add in high-stakes testing and (often) intense political engagement, and you've created a pressure cooker—with the CEO of the school system inside.

However, in spite of all those tough challenges, superintendents, informed observers, and those who have studied superintendent turnover in depth will tell you that **the underlying reason for most superintendent turnover is a breakdown in the board-superintendent relationship.** Many superintendents lament their "bad boards," "bad board behavior," or "crazy board members." They may feel their board "micro-manages," or they may be disheartened by the quality or philosophies of new members coming onto the board.

There are a few facts that need to be acknowledged up front:
- Superintendents may subtly influence (but rarely get to decide) who serves on their boards.

- Board members, in the majority of instances, are individuals who have little or no experience with governance or running an organization—let alone the largest and most complex organization in their community.
- Board members often come to their role owing someone (other than kids) for their help in getting them elected.
- Board members most often do not run for election on the platform of wanting to keep everything in the district exactly as it is; they usually run on some sort of agenda for change.
- While there is high turnover in the superintendency, the rapid rate of turnover among board members has created its own separate set of challenges for superintendents and school systems.

Having said that, based upon years of experience in working with hundreds of boards and superintendents all across the country, plus my own experience as a board member, superintendent and college president, I've concluded that the biggest barriers to making the board/CEO relationship work are as follows:

- The lack of *ownership of responsibility* on the part of the CEO for helping the governance team to be as effective as it can possibly be.
- The lack of *skill development* of superintendents in helping the governance team to be effective.
- The lack of personal capacity on the part of superintendents to effectively manage the complex relationships involved in having between 3 and 12 bosses.
- The lack of respect some superintendents demonstrate toward the board and its role in district leadership.
- The lack of creation, execution, and continuous maintenance of the framework, policies, procedures, and protocols necessary for the board/superintendent relationship to be successful. This includes a lack of clarity around decision-making authority.
- The lack of development of (and commitment to) an ongoing learning curriculum for the continuous improvement of the governance team.

Please don't misunderstand—I am a strong advocate for legislative change (as some states have adopted) to more clearly define the board's role and its key responsibilities of:

- policy-making

- defining success for the system
- monitoring progress against that defined success
- hiring, supporting, and holding the superintendent accountable for district performance within the context of state and local realities

But even within our existing governance structures, the majority of superintendents can assume more responsibility, develop greater skills, and be far more proactive in helping their entire governance team develop into a peak performing body. Remember, when superintendents are selected, they join the governance team—not as its owner or chief critic, but as a *member of the team*. Regardless of the educational level, experience, or capabilities of board members, governance is still a shared responsibility.

Other authors have written eloquently on the topic of public sector governance, presenting fully-developed philosophies and models. John Carver (Policy Governance) and Don McAdams (Reform Governance) come to mind as two of the best. Numerous successful board members, superintendents, associations, and consultants have authored their top "tips and tricks" for working with a board. These have also, for the most part, been helpful.

This book focuses on a comprehensive set of *practical strategies and a structural framework* that will help ensure that the governance team's focus and "constructive behavior" becomes a permanent way of doing business on behalf of the children they are there to serve.

While this book is written primarily as a tool for K-12 school superintendents, it should also be a must-read for anyone aspiring to that role, for members of the superintendent's leadership team, and for school board members interested in creating a governance team that works at an optimal level for the benefit of their children.

In the Arena

It is not the critic who counts, not the man who points how the strong man stumbled or where the doer of deeds could have done them better.

The credit belongs to the man who is actually in the arena; whose face is marred by dust and sweat and blood;

who strives valiantly; who errs and comes short again and again;

who knows the great enthusiasms, the great devotions, and spends himself in a worthy cause;

who, at the best, knows the triumph of high achievement;

and who, at the worst, if he fails, at least fails while daring greatly, so that his place shall never be with those cold and timid souls who know neither victory nor defeat.

Theodore Roosevelt, 1910

Acknowledgements

Any knowledge or wisdom presented in this book is a direct result of the experiences I've had in working with superintendents, boards, consultants, and, most importantly, great educational leaders. You all know who you are.

The opportunity to work with these leaders, learn from their experience, and observe them on the job both up close and from afar (at their very best, and sometimes when they've been something less than they aspired to be) has provided some of the richest learning of my career.

The credit does truly go to those "in the arena." We hope that the information provided herein, based on their experiences, makes the arena a little less "dusty, sweaty, and bloody" for those who will follow.

I'd like to thank several "critical friends" who reviewed early stages of this book and provided feedback and suggestions that have significantly enhanced the final product: Jim McIntyre, Pablo Munoz, Carl Harris, Jim Huge, Melody Johnson, Heath Morrison, and Larry Rowedder.

Thanks, also, to our editor, John Bebow, for his great work in helping us with this writing.

And I'd also like to acknowledge my life partner, business partner, and co-author on this project, Shelley Keith.

Introduction

Ask any superintendent, and they will tell you that working with the board is one of the most important, challenging, frustrating, and, at times, rewarding aspects of the job. The number one, fundamental reason superintendents leave their positions is because of the board—either an outright rift has developed between one or more of them and the superintendent, the board and the relationship are slowly making a turn for the worse, or the superintendent has simply become "tired" of dealing with the board.

> *"God made idiots—that was for practice. Then he made school boards."*
> *(Mark Twain)*

Becoming a superintendent is akin to entering into a professional "marriage" with three to twelve uniquely different individuals—with the superintendent's contract serving as the pre-nuptial agreement. Making this relationship work is always a complex challenge. Even if the district is blessed with a "good board," it can take a lot of time and effort to keep the superintendent/board relationship on track and the governance team working effectively. Plus, board membership changes over time, creating changing team dynamics that require continual attention.

> *"If you, as superintendent, adopt the Mark Twain perspective, then guess what—they're your idiots. Now, how are you going to help them be effective for the system and its kids?"*
> *(Tim Quinn)*

While some superintendents in some states are elected to their roles by the public or appointed by a mayor or county executive, the vast majority of our country's 15,000+ superintendents are selected, appointed, and evaluated by a school board. A handful of these boards are appointed by public officials, but the majority of board members are elected by the public. Their names have been placed on the ballot, they have campaigned for office, and they have won the popular vote of their voting constituents. In many cases, they have been endorsed by (and perhaps have accepted campaign contributions from) various constituent groups whose interests may or may not be aligned with the best interests of their community's children.

I share all of this because it is the backdrop for this complex and challenging partnership between the board and the superintendent, or what I'll refer to throughout as *the governance team.*

The Governance <u>Team</u>

Let's take a minute to define the term "governance team." I call it a team, rather than a committee or governing body, to reflect the fact that teams are groups of people organized to work together toward common ends. **The governance team includes the elected or appointed members of the board <u>plus</u> the superintendent.** Without the board, the superintendent is simply the superintendent, managing the operational aspects of the district. Without the superintendent, the board is simply the board, providing oversight on behalf of the community. **Together, they comprise the governance *team*—a team that, if working effectively, has great potential to do good for children and the community.**

The governance team also includes anyone else who, by law, reports directly to the board. In some states, Chief Financial Officers report directly to the board and effectively become members of "the team." Also included are any members of the superintendent's leadership team that the superintendent chooses to invite into the relationship, either on a permanent or ad hoc basis. It does <u>not</u> include the district's legal counsel or the person who takes minutes at board meetings. The superintendent/board relationship is complex at best. I strongly encourage superintendents and boards to be very thoughtful and cautious regarding expansion of governance team membership. The more personalities involved, the more complex and challenging the dynamics become.

I must note here that, over time, I have observed an increasing number of governance teams treat their district attorneys as ad hoc board members. The attorneys have subtlety convinced the boards that, by being in attendance at every meeting, they can keep the board from harm (and perhaps also protect their political interests.) Not only does this become expensive for the district, it undermines the role of the superintendent. The role of the district's legal counsel is to advise on *legal* issues (when asked), and not to advise on educational policy or politics on an ongoing basis.

Let me provide a couple of examples at the extreme ends of the governance team spectrum, where the board and superintendent have and have not historically worked as a team. First is Kansas City, Missouri—a district that has been in turmoil at the top of the organization for over thirty years. Between the late 1970's and 2008, the board hired and either fired or chased off 26 different superintendents. I'm not suggesting that the board was always wrong, but the level of dysfunction at the top of that organization also resulted in the loss of over 60,000 students—from almost 80,000 to less than 20,000. It also resulted in the loss and waste of hundreds of millions of taxpayer dollars, the loss of faith and support of parents and community, and a well-deserved reputation as one of the very worst school systems in the country. It appears that as of 2008, this system has begun to demonstrate a dramatic turnaround. If the superintendent and board can remain focused and committed to working together, better things are in store for their system, their community's children, and their community at large.

At the other end of that spectrum is Gwinnett County, Georgia, where the board and the same superintendent have been working in concert and as a team for almost two decades. During that time, the district has experienced exponential growth, now serving over 160,000 students, plus an incredible increase in the ethnic and socioeconomic diversity of their student body. Those two forces, in many instances, could have been a recipe for conflict, chaos, and declining student performance. Not, however, in Gwinnett County. To the contrary, both their board and superintendent have been recognized nationally for their outstanding leadership. Most importantly, the district won the coveted $1 million Broad Prize in 2010 for being the urban district that has done the best job in the country in raising achievement levels of all children and closing achievement gaps between ethnic and socioeconomic groups.

What About Boards Has Recently Changed?

At key intervals over the past decade, we have had the opportunity to interview over 150 school superintendents from around the country about various aspects of their jobs. Generally, superintendents believe that local school boards, in general, have experienced significant change in recent years in terms of composition, focus, and aspiration. When asked what, specifically, has changed about school boards, the most frequent responses included:

- Fewer community leaders are willing to serve on school boards.
- There are more single-issue candidates running for board seats, focused on one (often self-serving) issue, and boards are more political in nature.
- More board members are coming with wrong motives; they may want to get someone hired, get someone fired, get some specific vendor a contract, or enhance their own name recognition in preparation for a run for higher elective office.
- More former fired or retired school district employees are being elected to the board.
- Few newly elected members come with any significant understanding of the appropriate role of a public board, or of the complexity of running a large organization.
- There are more members for whom this is the most important activity in their lives, and their new role becomes an all-consuming part of their daily activities—often to the detriment of the superintendent and his/her team.
- Voter turnout for board elections in many communities is typically very low, resulting in school employees having a disproportionate say in electing their own "bosses," or other interest groups in electing representatives of their own sometimes narrow interests.

Under the **BEST** of circumstances, the board will be comprised of quality individuals who are dedicated to the interests of children, understand governance, and have the leadership skills to handle their roles in an effective manner that provides a positive example for everyone in the system. Under the **BEST** of circumstances, the board will have elected a wise, trusted, and effective leader as its president or chair. Unfortunately, this **"best of circumstances"** scenario seems to occur less frequently and is not necessarily the norm today.

The Governance Team "Coach"

Therefore, superintendents who find themselves in less than the best of circumstances need to adopt the role of "First Teacher" of the organization. Although a wise superintendent would never pronounce this to his or her board, the superintendent must, all too often, (sometimes by default) quietly assume the role of governance team "coach." The superintendent is the professional educator and board members are the lay citizen owner-trustees of the system who bring varying levels of interest, knowledge, and expertise to their roles. *It is the superintendent's job to help board members grow in their roles and become the most effective governance team they can be for the children of the community.* The

purpose of the information presented herein is to help superintendents become more effective in this role and to provide the governance team with a structural framework within which they can successfully conduct their business.

> *"When things are going well, look out the window. When there are difficulties, look in the mirror."*
> *(Jim Collins)*

I have seen a number of superintendents who, finding themselves in a situation that was not the "best of circumstances," immediately plunge into "Woe is me!" mode. Out of self-pity or a stubborn denial that "this is not part of my job," they refused to *own* the situation and refused to own the work of helping the governance team become better. Others have tried to delegate working with the board to other staff members. These approaches did not serve their system, its children, their board, or their careers very well. Success for a system and its children is predicated to a large degree on the long-term success of the governance team. Superintendents really *don't have a choice* but to "own" and help lead the team toward that success. Building the governance team is a required and primary ongoing component of the superintendent's job.

What's In This Book

Having had the opportunity to observe hundreds of these professional "marriages" and witness their natural ups and downs, I've developed a set of very practical and useful strategies for helping superintendents and boards manage this partnership. What is presented is more than a set of "tips and tricks" for working with a board. It is a *structure* that can help keep the team pointed in the same direction and help keep the "marriage" on track and prospering.

Following these practices can also help superintendents be far more productive (on behalf of children) in the use of their time. Some superintendents report that they spend up to one-third or even one-half of their time each week on activities related to the "care and feeding" of their boards. Unfortunately, most of this time is not focused on activity related to improving student achievement, which must be the core function of any successful system.

Please recognize that everything offered here may not be appropriate in every situation. Superintendents need to be cognizant of local history and context in planning their approach. If, for example, the district has a "best of circumstances" board, the superintendent may simply need to just support the board leadership in fulfilling governance team responsibilities.

This book is presented in four main chapters. Sample or model documents and the tools referenced within each chapter are provided in the Appendices. **Readers should not assume that "this is all I need," because it isn't.** For governance teams to be as successful as they need to be, the superintendent and each member of the team need to become avid students of the discipline of GOVERNANCE and make a commitment to continuous development in their roles.

The information is presented as follows:

Governance Team Basics
This chapter provides a useful mental model for thinking about the appropriate responsibilities, composition, and behavior of the governance team and its members.

Governance Team Foundational Elements
This chapter focuses on the key policies, practices, processes, and protocols that should be in place to define and clarify working relationships between and among governance team members.

The Governance Team in Action
The conduct of governance team business, including the effective execution of board meetings, is critical to team success. This chapter addresses strategies and tools that will be helpful in the successful conduct of business.

Attracting and Retaining Quality Board Members
This chapter addresses strategies for ensuring that quality people who appropriately represent the interests of children and the community serve on the board.

Is your governance team leadership as good as your children deserve? If you know your team can be more effective, read on.

Governance Team Basics

As stated in the Introduction, the board and the superintendent, together, comprise the governance team and need to work together as a team if the district is going to be as successful as it can be in its work on behalf of children. As Don McAdams says, *if there is chaos in the board room, there will – in time – be chaos in the classroom.* The superintendent without the board is simply the CEO. The board without the superintendent is simply the board. Collectively, you comprise the governance team, which can be a powerful force for children when performing at its peak.

Peak Performing Governance Teams

Over years of study and work with many boards, I've observed five basic characteristics of peak performing governance teams.

1. *Team members are united by their commitment to the service of children.*

   Whether elected or appointed, team members come with one pure primary motive—to serve the best interests of children. They are not there to advance their political careers or to advance a personal ideological agenda. They are not there to get someone hired, or get someone fired. They are not there to advocate for individuals, single demographic groups, or groups of adults. They focus the vast majority of their attention, time and discussions on what is best for all students. They care about the development of the "whole child," but place greatest focus on the academic success of children. Their first and last priority is to represent the interests of children, especially those with no other strong voice within the context of the school community.

   > *"Whatever you do unto the least of these, so also you do unto me"*
   > *(Matthew 25:40)*

Effective governance teams are mindful that all of the children who walk through your doors have different levels of voice. By this I mean they have different levels of power and representation—based on who they are, the families they come from, whether their parents happen to know a teacher, whether they even have parents. All of these factors have an influence on a child's status and voice within the institution. Peak performing governance teams assume the responsibility of serving as advocate for every single child, especially those with little or no voice. There are many times when the interests of adults are expressed in the loudest and most persistent voice. Some of these interests may be inconsistent with the best interests of all children.

For example, in recent years, a number of governance teams I have worked with have taken on the "sacred cow" of teacher seniority in staff assignments. For decades, common contract language or board policy has basically allowed the most senior, and often the best, teachers to choose the least challenging teaching assignments—often in the more affluent schools and usually with kids who need their talents the least. The proposed change was to make sure that the students with the greatest needs received the best and most experienced teachers. Not a one who has taken on this issue did so to the applause of the adults within the system. But they clearly understood that their job was to advocate for the children first, even when it meant dealing with the firestorm of adult interests.

2. *The board and the superintendent have an _interdependent_ relationship.*

Everyone on the team understands the "ownership" role of the board and the "professional management" role of the superintendent. Neither party should be overly dependent upon the other, nor operate totally independently of the other.

Many superintendents like to keep their boards dependent upon them, or controlled by them. If the superintendent is very talented, this may work in the short run, but isn't good for the district or its clients in the long run. Boards need to know what their job is and how to do it without depending upon the superintendent to do their job for them.

I have seen capable superintendents who asked their boards to simply allow them to manage the organization and hold them accountable, which was fine. But then their Type A personalities kicked into gear, and they jumped into doing a good share of the board's policy work and community engagement work as well. While this worked well in the short term, it did not help their successors, who needed strong boards at some point during their tenure. Instead of promoting the development of strong and capable boards, the superintendents had allowed the boards to become overly dependent upon them.

By the same token, many superintendents become overly dependent upon their boards. They don't have the strength to make tough management decisions, so they engage the board on matters that aren't at a board policy level. I've seen many examples of this, usually with beginning superintendents (or with "Peter Principle" superintendents) who lack the confidence, courage, and experience to keep the board focused on their own work. This leads to long meetings, a proliferation of board committees, micromanagement, and the involvement of the board in decisions that they should never, ever be asked to make. For the most part, board members have neither the professional expertise nor the time to manage the district on a day-to-day basis. Once the board has jumped into day-to-day operations, it is hard for them to get back out of that "box." They also lose their perspective and focus as overseers and evaluators of district progress, focusing instead on daily management matters.

> *"A board and superintendent united in their efforts to work together will produce the kind of school system our children deserve."*
> *(Kentucky Board Member)*

Likewise, no one on the governance team should act like a "lone ranger," operating completely <u>independently</u> of the others. All members need to respect the others, keep them informed, and seek each others' advice and counsel on key issues. All too often, we see individuals elected to boards who believe it is their responsibility to be the "anti-" member—anti-superintendent, anti-governance team, anti-status quo—pick your flavor. They are not interested in developing any functional working relationships with their fellow board members or the superintendent. They believe they are there to "shake things up."

These lone rangers may play to the applause of a limited constituency, but the fact of the matter is that they rarely get anything positive accomplished for the district. Their "acting out" in public often hurts the district and lowers its credibility in the community. If the governance team wants to make good things happen for kids, <u>they all</u> need to work together in some spirit of cooperation.

Finding the right, *inter*dependent balance involves a combination of factors, including the competence and experience of the superintendent, the competence and experience of the board, the trust and confidence the board has in the superintendent and his or her leadership team, and the commitment that the superintendent and board chair have made to the continuing growth and development of fellow team members.

3. *Indicators of success are established for the district.*

The governance team has adopted statements of mission, vision, and guiding principles for the district. They have clearly articulated indicators of success and have identified how success will be measured. Specific responsibilities for the achievement of that success have also been established for the board, superintendent, staff and community. Everyone knows where the organization is going, how they'll know if they're getting there, and who is responsible for the strategic initiatives designed to get there. They have also developed and clearly articulated the consequences for results—good or bad. Accountability starts at the very top and cascades throughout the entire organization. Wherever this is not adopted as a basic governing premise, the majority of the district's children seldom get what they ultimately need or deserve.

Establishing these metrics of success can help keep a governance team focused on what is important. Every issue before the board can be evaluated in terms of its impact on these indicators.

> *"Board meetings are not about running an organization but about what the organization should be running toward."*
> *(John Carver)*

Let me add a couple of key caveats to this discussion. First, it never ceases to amaze me how many governance teams have confused *success* with *compliance* (with state or federal regulations or standards.) In most instances, state and federal standards are set too low to ensure that children have the knowledge they need to be successful competitors in the global economy. And, few state or federal standards at the time of this publication even hint at what success means in any comprehensive way, nor what it means for the rest of a district's functional areas of service such as Operations, Human Resources, etc., etc.

> *"Trust is the lubricant that makes it possible for organizations to work."*
> *(Warren Bennis)*

Second, when governance teams fail to step up and define success for the system, everyone else in the system defines success in their own terms. When that happens, anything anyone does is OK, and anything anyone does is subject to question and challenge. Establishing metrics of success, and a parallel accountability plan, is one of the governance team's most critical responsibilities.

4. *Governance team relationships are based upon trust and respect.*

The governance team owes it to the taxpayers and the children of the district to be the most effective governing body they can possibly be. This doesn't mean that everyone will always agree—there will (and should) be healthy disagreements along the way. But it also doesn't mean that governance team members should have free reign to "act out" in public. A good challenge for your team is that every meeting could serve as an outstanding example for the 9th grade civics class of how democracy should work at its best. The job is too important to let the team devolve into petty personal disputes and lack of trust.

If your board meetings are televised and are the best reality TV show on the air, you've got a problem. This has a negative impact on the district's image, which will eventually begin to impact enrollment or the ability to pass critical ballot issues. **Governance team behavior sets the tone for the entire district. How members conduct their business matters greatly in establishing the culture and the tone for the manner in which work is conducted throughout the entire system—from classrooms to kitchens to the bus garage.**

Trust—in the governance team setting—means knowing what you can expect from your team mates. You trust that if they have a problem with you, they will talk to you about it face-to-face in private, not in public. You trust that if a colleague does not agree with you on an issue, they will discuss it with you in a respectful manner. They won't surprise you, "hijack" you, or disrespect you in public. They will listen to you and try to understand your viewpoint, even if they may disagree with you in the final analysis.

Governance team members must also respect the differences in what each of them brings to the table in terms of skills and interests. One member may be passionately interested in teaching and learning, while another may have a deep interest in the finances. They find ways to respect and support each others' needs and honor the strengths that they bring to the team.

One new superintendent, with whom I worked closely, discovered, to her chagrin, that board meetings were rather uncivil in her new district. Board members were disrespectful towards each other and towards staff making presentations, using board meetings as opportunities to "score points" with their constituents by making rude comments to others. At the next board retreat, the superintendent noted that these types of comments were not tolerated by students or teachers in the classrooms, and may, in fact, even be considered bullying behavior. She noted that this was setting a bad example for the children in the district and reminded them that something more is expected from people governing an organization dedicated to the development of children. The board discussed the problem, and adopted new standards of practice for how they would handle and process disagreements. They also delegated responsibility for enforcement of their new standards to a well-respected veteran board member. The situation improved quickly and holds as of this writing.

5. *The governance team has developed strong and durable linkages with the community.*

The team understands that they are the "owners" of the district on behalf of the community. Therefore, they have established avenues for regular, meaningful dialog with the community regarding district directions—outside of normal board meetings. They are proactive, not reactive, in seeking community perspectives on key decisions that are on the horizon. Formal and informal intentional communication with the community must occur.

The board expects that the superintendent and the superintendent's leadership team will make the provision of quality services to their constituents a priority, and that well-defined channels for problem-resolution are available to the public. But, the board also understands that ultimate policy decisions are theirs, morally and legally, and don't abdicate those responsibilities to any interest group.

Often times in our work with challenged boards, we'll get push-back on these characteristics. It will usually be something like, "Isn't this all a bit idealistic?" My answer, of course, is always ***absolutely!*** Governance teams need to understand that if they want the district—with its all-important mission of developing the community's children—to aspire to high ideals, those high ideals begin at the top of the organization, with the board. Then, they work to live up to those ideals in the conduct of their business. There is no other forum where being "idealistic" in thought and deed is more appropriate or more important.

Useful Models of Governance

There are two prominent and especially useful governance models in use today—the Policy Governance Model and the Reform Governance Model. Both can provide useful mental models in thinking about the roles and relationships between the superintendent and the board. A brief summary of each is provided below.

Policy Governance Model

One of the best thinkers on the topic of public board governance is John Carver, who developed the Policy Governance Model. Even if your board doesn't fully adopt the "Carver Model," it is worth studying as it provides an excellent mental framework for the conduct of the board's business.

I'll briefly summarize and paraphrase the basic concepts of the Carver Model as they apply to school systems, with apologies to John Carver for anything I may have interpreted differently than intended. (You should definitely study these concepts directly from the source.)

Carver says that boards govern through policy, and they develop policy in four areas:

1. *The Board's Processes*: These are the basic understandings of how the board will conduct its business—board bylaws, role of officers, how members are replaced who resign mid-term, how meetings are conducted, how situations are handled such as violation of the confidence of closed sessions, ethics policies, etc.

> *"Perfection of means and confusion of ends seems to characterize our age."*
> *(Albert Einstein)*

2. *The Board-CEO Relationship*: These are understandings the board has with the superintendent. Many items will be covered in the superintendent's contract, but there may be other policies relating to how the superintendent is evaluated, standards of governance team practice, communication protocols, etc. Carver makes it clear that the board has a supervisory relationship with only one staff member—and that's the superintendent.

3. *Ends*: These policies establish the purpose and intended outcomes of the organization. They define the district's mission, vision, indicators of success, metrics, and how people will be held accountable.

4. *Means*: These policies establish limitations on the superintendent's and staff's autonomy in achieving the district's ends. Carver encourages boards to prescribe the Ends, but provide as much autonomy and do as little micromanaging as possible regarding the Means.

Carver establishes several key principles about governance. Again, these are paraphrased for the superintendency:

1. The Board "owns" the organization as elected representatives of the community, to whom it is accountable. Therefore, the primary relationship the board has is with the community—not the staff, students or faculty.

2. The Board employs a superintendent, with whom it shares the ownership, and to whom it delegates leadership responsibility and the day-to-day management of the district.

3. The superintendent is the only employee of the district who reports to the board, receives direction from the board, and is evaluated by the board. (Note: State law, in some instances, may dictate that the district's chief financial officer or attorney report directly to the board as well.)

4. The Board speaks with one voice or none at all. Individual trustees or board committees have no authority over the district—only by acting as a body is board authority expressed. Once a vote is taken,

the board has spoken and decisions must be supported as decided. (When interviewed by the media, board members may state that while they did not vote for a particular decision, now that the matter is decided, they support the decision of the board.)

5.   The Board should prescribe the ends for the district, but stay out of the means. Board leadership is best expressed by articulating what the district is to achieve for its community, and evaluating progress toward those ends—not by becoming immersed in the day-to-day operation of the district.

6.   The Board holds the superintendent accountable for progress toward its identified indicators of success or ends.

7.   Performance of the superintendent must be monitored, but only against established criteria.

8.   The superintendent recognizes the board's need to receive adequate and timely information for decision-making and for monitoring improvement on the indicators of success.

9.   The superintendent must assume responsibility for engagement of faculty and staff in the planning and decision-making processes, to the extent necessary to ensure quality decisions, ownership and successful implementation.

10.   The Board and the superintendent are jointly responsible for developing and maintaining effective processes for communication, decision-making, and handling of issues that may come before the Board.

Fully adopting Carver's Policy Governance Model will normally require a significant commitment of time and focus on the part of a board. Most often, the help of a skilled facilitator is required. However, many governance teams who have committed to this model have become high-functioning governance teams. (Refer to www.policygovernance.com for more information.)

Another great resource, particularly for urban school boards, is the Reform Governance model developed by Don McAdams, former president of the Houston Independent School District and founder of the Center for Reform of School Systems (CRSS). In his book <u>What School Boards Can Do:</u> <u>Reform Governance for Urban Schools,</u> McAdams outlines a framework for the key responsibilities of boards. He states that reform governance is governance for a purpose, not just governance as a process.

McAdams' framework states that there is a "line" between the work of the board (above the line) and the work of the superintendent (below the line.) Sometimes this can seem like a wavy line, but is a useful analogy just the same.

In a nutshell, the key components of board work (above the line) include:
- Core Beliefs and Commitments – stating what the board believes about children and public schools; what their commitments are to the children
- Theories of Action for Change – agreeing upon what strategies the board believes will create a high-performing district
- Reform Policies – adopting policies that support the board's Theory of Action to create a high-performing school system
- Policy Development and Oversight – adopting operating policies for the district, focusing on the ends rather than the means
- Roles, Responsibilities and Relationships – defining appropriate roles for the board and their relationships with the community; agreeing on appropriate channels for providing service to constituents
- Building Blocks of Reform Governance – defining the major processes by which the board does their work—board meetings, workshops, ad hoc committees, roles of officers, agenda development, etc.
- Building Civic Capacity – providing leadership in the community that supports building a high-performing district
- Transition Planning – managing the succession of board members and superintendents to ensure high-quality, committed people serve on the governance team

Governance team training utilizing this framework is available through CRSS, www.crss.org.

Governance Team Foundational Elements

When invited in to help resolve problems within governance teams, I often observe that the governance team has neglected to adopt some foundational policies, processes, protocols and understandings that could have been very helpful in preventing the problems that seem to loom so large in their current state of challenge or dysfunction.

Most of these foundational elements are so simple, or commonsensical, that they are often overlooked and taken for granted. But when they are not in place, there is no point of reference to return to for guidance and no framework for the manner in which all team members have agreed to conduct their business. In some instances, these elements have been adopted, but between turnover on the board and/or in the superintendency, they have simply been forgotten or are no longer followed. Once in place, taking time periodically to review, discuss and update these elements can help to fine-tune the inner working of the governance team.

> *"The problems with boards are failures of processes, not failures of people."*
> *(John Carver)*

Over the years, I've concluded that there are eight key elements that can be most helpful in providing a strong foundation for a superintendent's relationship with their board:

- Position descriptions for the board and for the superintendent
- Superintendent's contract language, specifically outlining management authority
- Performance evaluation processes for the superintendent <u>and</u> for the governance team
- Board member oath of office
- Governance team standards of practice
- Governance team communication protocols
- Quarterly board retreats
- A "Kitchen Cabinet" for the superintendent

Position Descriptions

It is helpful to articulate the "job" of the board. The majority of people coming to board service do not have a clear understanding of their new role and its responsibilities. Both boards and superintendents can sometimes have a hard time determining the difference between governance and management, and identifying a policy issue versus a management issue.

Typical board duties include:
- Define vision, mission, and indicators of success for the district
- Adopt a district plan, then monitor and evaluate progress on the plan
- Hire, compensate, support, and evaluate the superintendent, and hold the superintendent accountable for achieving success as defined
- Adopt a responsible district budget aligned with the district plan and indicators of success
- Establish appropriate district policies
- Proactively engage the community on critical decisions as appropriate
- Ensure the district provides appropriate service to constituents
- Model professional development and continuous learning in the board role
- Be publicly accountable for the success of the district as defined
- Model professional behavior in the conduct of the district's business
- Serve as advocates for the interests of children before advocating for the interests of any adult interest groups

The duties of the superintendent are often articulated by state statute or in the superintendent's contract. Typical superintendent duties include:
- Manage the day-to-day operations as CEO of the district, focusing on achievement of the vision, mission, and indicators of success
- Function as the primary advisor to and full non-voting member of the governance team
- Effectively communicate with and support the board

- Manage the development of, and recommend for board approval, a coherent, comprehensive strategic plan; then implement the district's adopted plan
- Establish an aligned accountability plan for all district, school, and department employees
- Prepare, align, propose, and monitor the budget
- Hire and develop great staff; terminate incompetent or unwilling staff
- Proactively engage parents and the community as appropriate
- Be publicly accountable for the success of the district as defined by the board
- Recognize and assume the role of 1st learner, 1st teacher, 1st advocate for children, and 1st collaborator on their behalf

The point here is that if you don't have the job descriptions, get them in place. Use them in new board member training and as part of the performance assessment process for both the board and the superintendent.

See Appendix A for sample board and superintendent position descriptions.

The Superintendent's Contract

In addition to the typical contract clauses regarding compensation, renewal, nonrenewal, etc., the superintendent's contract should clarify the respective roles of the superintendent and the board. (See our book *The Superintendent Search Process: Getting the Job and Getting Off to a Great Start* for more information on the superintendent's contract.)

Language should also be included in the superintendent's contract stating that the only time the board meets without the superintendent is during discussions of his/her performance and compensation.

If the board has a history of meddling in the rightful responsibilities of the superintendent, superintendents and boards should be open to including a "no meddling clause" in the contract, stating explicitly what the board will not do. In extreme situations, it may also be appropriate to include consequences for board violation of these contract provisions. **See Appendix B for examples of language for these types of provisions.**

While clauses of this type are not common, in some circumstances they may be necessary—if only to capture the attention of the board and place them on notice regarding the consequences of inappropriate behavior. It's not likely that a first-time superintendent (unless that person is a well-known peak performer) would be successful in negotiating this type of language. More often, we've seen similar language in the case of a reputable and experienced superintendent taking the reins of an extremely troubled district.

Performance Evaluation of the Superintendent and Governance Team

The superintendent's contract may, at best, outline an evaluation process or, at least, commit to a timeline for establishing an evaluation process, which would then be included in a later addendum to the contract or adopted as board policy. See our book *The Superintendent Search Process: A Guide to Getting the Job and Getting Off to a Great Start* for a more complete discussion of the superintendent's performance evaluation.

It is important at this time to get an agreement that the entire governance team will assess *its* performance on a regular basis as well. I've seen boards take the attitude that their evaluation is simple—it is done by the electorate every time their name appears on the ballot. They fail to understand, however, that the evaluation process isn't just a means of judging performance, but an opportunity for reflection, dialog, professional growth and organizational development.

I've also seen governance teams take this responsibility very seriously, making a commitment to regularly discuss their own performance and provide the superintendent with formative feedback on a regular basis as well. It simply goes back to the concept that **people are at their best when they are growing or helping others grow. Board members have to make a commitment to both if they are going to fulfill their responsibilities to the children their system was established to serve.**

A simple, yet effective, self-assessment rubric could be established based upon the board's job description, the governance team standards of practice, their adopted communication protocols, the five characteristics of Peak Performing Governance teams outlined herein, or some combination of each. **See Appendix I for sample tools for getting the dialog started around governance team assessment.**

Quarterly Board Retreats

It is best to get agreement between the board and the superintendent during the contract negotiation process that the "team" will meet on a regular basis to provide formative performance assessments. I support quarterly retreats. These quarterly performance assessments, which in most states can be held in executive session, provide the opportunity to discuss progress on district initiatives and obtain formative feedback from the board. Again, refer to our book *The Superintendent Search Process: A Guide to Getting the Job and Getting Off to a Great Start* for further explanation and detail on the use of this retreat. Suffice it to say that if the superintendent's evaluation is going to be a *process* rather than a once per year *event,* the board needs to reserve the time in advance to do it well. In some districts, a quarterly retreat may not be possible. The key point, however, is to commit to regular retreats, as often as needed, to ensure effective communication about district progress, performance of the superintendent, and the performance of the governance team—which has significant impact on the performance of the superintendent and the superintendent's staff.

One example of the strategic use of board retreats came while I was serving as a board member for a private, not-for-profit organization. I had the opportunity to interview a candidate for the CEO position who had an extensive background in the private sector, including serving as CEO of a large utility company. When asked about board relationships, she provided an answer that provided an epiphany in my thinking about how to make a governance team work. She explained that as she began in this assignment, during her first year she would request a minimum of one day in retreat for every member of the board. For example, if she had a seven member board, she wanted seven days committed to board retreats. She also went on to say that any time new members joined the board, the entire board should meet the same number of days in retreat as there were new members. Her point was that it was important to take the time to orient new board members to their role, review operating and communication protocols with the whole board, and review and recommit to or modify their strategic plan, including the board's indicators of success. This was a non-negotiable element of her governance team equation—one that makes a lot of sense in ensuring ongoing understanding of and commitment to the concept of effective governance.

Standards of Practice

Each governance team should develop their own "code of conduct." These may also be called ground rules or standards of practice. They are affirmations and aspirations of ideal team member behavior. Some boards also adopt a code of ethics. **See Appendix C for a set of model standards of practice.** Most standards will include statements such as:

"True friends stab you in the front."
(Oscar Wilde)

- All decisions will be based on what's good for children.
- Members will not use their positions for personal gain.
- The board will focus on policy work and not the day-to-day operations.
- Members will always treat each other with respect in public.
- Members will properly handle or refer any complaints or issues to the superintendent or designee for resolution.
- Members will maintain the confidentiality of closed session information.

Thoughtful superintendents may also choose to adopt a similar set of standards of practice with their leadership teams, so the entire district leadership structure is operating with similar understandings about the manner in which district business will be conducted.

Oath of Office

The standards of practice may then be written into an Oath of Office **(see sample in Appendix D)** for newly elected or re-elected board members. Some boards reaffirm their standards of practice at the beginning of every meeting. Some governance teams reaffirm their oath of office at the annual organizational meeting. Taking an oath that includes the education of a community's children is serious business and should not be taken lightly.

Communication Protocols

Communication protocols are another useful tool **(see sample in Appendix E).** These spell out mutual understandings and expectations about how the board and superintendent will:
- Keep each other informed
- Handle their differences
- Communicate with each other (specific communication channels)
- Handle requests for information
- Respond to complaints or problems
- Support each other in public

Communication with the board is an important part of a superintendent's responsibilities. With today's technologies, there are many easy ways to accomplish timely communication about items of importance and interest to board members. I have seen too many instances where a superintendent was doing everything right in the area of student achievement, but was in poor favor with the board—the root cause of which was lack of effective communication about what was going on in the district.

The board should also adopt **enforcement provisions** for their standards and protocols. The board president or the president's designee should be specifically charged with enforcing the standards of practice, protocols and board policies. In some cases, the district legal counsel is asked to play this role. There should be increasing sanctions of members for repeated or serious offenses. Most public bodies, even the U.S. Senate, have provisions for sanctioning members for egregious behavior. The work of school boards is the most critical public work at the local level—why wouldn't sanctions for violation of policy or inappropriate behavior apply here, as well? **See Appendix F for a sample board policy covering board member violation of policy.**

One large urban district in the South has perhaps the most comprehensive code of ethics policy that I've seen with respect to governance team behavior. It is clear, concise, and addresses in advance the behaviors and issues that can drive superintendents to distraction and governance teams to dysfunction. By policy, the responsibility for enforcement of the ethics policy is delegated to the district's general counsel. Any time a board member "steps over the line," they receive a call from the general counsel's office to schedule a meeting to discuss the infraction. In instances where the behavior is repeated, the consequences increase correspondingly.

Kitchen Cabinet

Wise leaders seek the independent and private counsel of other leaders, influencers, or experts. They create an unofficial "Kitchen Cabinet" in order to:
- Gain perspective on issues
- Expand their knowledge and political awareness in the context of this community
- Help evaluate ideas, develop strategies and probe problems
- Seek unique viewpoints on old problems
- Seek new ideas
- Develop relationships that may be helpful in navigating political challenges

Most Kitchen Cabinets are never officially identified as such—except in the minds of the leaders who use them. The Kitchen Cabinet may never meet as a group and may never know who the other members are. In fact, any mention of such a group by the superintendent has the potential to create animosity within the system's formal leadership structure and among governance team members. But it is a rare district where the leadership and governance teams have all of the knowledge, influence and talent it will take to move the district forward. Those who rely only upon themselves, those they report to, and those who report to them for input run the risk that their stream of advisors will be too narrow, too shallow, or dominated by special interests. Therefore, the selection and effective use of a Kitchen Cabinet can be most helpful to the superintendent in achieving success for the system.

Some school superintendents are politically masterful and go about the process of developing a Kitchen Cabinet instinctively and informally, perhaps not even aware of what they are creating. Most need to be more deliberate in their actions, carefully selecting a well-rounded group of advisors. We suggest that superintendents attempt to balance the membership of this group with qualities or characteristics that may be missing from the staff or the board, i.e. diversity, age, occupation, etc.

Upon entering a district, the wise superintendent will get to know their board members and direct reports quickly and well. One-on-one interviews with each will provide volumes of information about the individual talents, values, and perspectives of the members. The interviews will also help identify others in the community who are seen as having expertise and insights which need to be cultivated by the superintendent. The astute superintendent will then use this information to develop a political map of the system. (Refer to our book *In the Arena* for more detail on the use of political mapping.)

Obviously, there is a premium on the superintendent's time, particularly in the first year on the job. While everyone wants to meet the new superintendent, the superintendent must be strategic about where to spend time in deep relational development. This time can be scheduled with an eye toward gaining exposure to the talent pool of the community and developing potential critical advisors and supporters.

The lesson here is that, while there may be five, seven or even a dozen board members, there is only one superintendent. The movers and shakers in the community want a relationship with the person who is CEO of their school system, and they can be very helpful in managing the sometimes delicate issues of community and board politics.

By the time the superintendent's first 90 days are completed, there should be a long list of potential advisors. By the time the first 180 days are completed and the strategic plan is in place, there should be a short list of key members who have been primed and ready to support the district's agenda on behalf of the community and its children.

Over time, and as the agenda and needs change, the Kitchen Cabinet will also change. But the superintendent should never short-change the power of their position in recruiting other community leaders to help in achieving system success. Effective boards can be helpful to superintendents in developing a well-rounded group of community advisors and influencers.

The Governance Team in Action

The board's work is conducted in public meetings. All too many superintendents will confide that board meetings are the least fun part of their jobs. Often, there is too much drama and wild card behavior that creates chaos and detracts from the district's positive image. All too often, a game of "gotcha" is played between board members or by board members in their interaction with district staff.

There are a few key tools peak performing governance teams use to help keep the board's work focused, efficient and effective:

"All it takes to create an asylum is an empty room and the right sort of people."
(My Man Godfrey)

- A dynamic plan and planning process
- An accountability system
- Annual board calendar
- Standard board agenda format and meeting protocols
- Specific and defined role for board president
- Protocols and standards for staff preparation of board meeting materials
- Protocols and standards for staff presentations at board meetings
- Board committee protocols
- Governance team professional development plan
- Media engagement protocols

Dynamic Plan and Planning Process

Nothing provides more focus for a board than to have a board-created, adopted, and owned dynamic district strategic plan that clearly defines success. Responsibility for achieving the defined outcomes of the plan, as well as consequences of performance (or non-performance,) are clearly defined. A strong strategic plan provides the basis for the board's policy work and the board's monitoring of superintendent and district performance. Everything the board considers should be weighed in the context of the plan and impact upon the district's defined indicators of success.

I've seen a number of superintendents enter districts that had some type of "strategic plan" in place that no one owned, few people understood, and fewer yet used it as a guide for their work. Often, there is nothing particularly compelling about existing plans, success is not clearly defined, and no system of accountability for results has been built in. In all too many cases, the plans were expensive to develop, look nice in a vinyl-bound notebook on the shelf or posted on the district's website, but are generally ignored. We call these "vinyl trophies." Districts that possess them have little focus.

> *"Good plans shape good decisions."*
> *(Lester Bittel)*

As noted earlier, I've also seen boards and superintendents completely abdicate responsibility for defining system success to either the state or federal government. They've confused a low bar of compliance with the higher bar of success that they want for their own kids. This is a flaw in thinking that can have a devastating impact on a system and its children.

Perhaps the most critical responsibility of the governance team, with input from the community, is to create that crystal-clear vision—a statement of the most ideal, conceivable and believable future—and then build a plan for getting there. Creating metrics for each functional area of the system, for every school, and every classroom, then being transparent about baseline data and results of efforts, literally sets the foundation for district transformation and student success.

Having a dynamic plan provides incredible opportunity for board focus. They can see how board agenda items relate to the bottom line and can conduct their decision-making based on how actions will support attainment of their vision and indicators of success. Reports to the board are no longer just for the sake of reporting—they focus on the district's status in achieving the outcome of the plan. Every board agenda item beyond the consent agenda should cite the specific success target or metric to which it pertains.

Accountability System

Accountability correlates closely with the dynamic plan. **The governance team must assume public and personal accountability for district success.** The superintendent must be provided the authority to lead and be supported by the board, then be held publicly accountable by the board for district success. This provides the foundation and the political cover for the superintendent to establish accountability for all other district staff. In the process, the district makes accountability data available to the public and easy to access.

This is one area where most districts struggle. This can be due to:
- lack of time committed to the planning process
- lack of specificity regarding what success means
- lack of quality data
- timidity about being publicly accountable and holding staff accountable

Until districts have well-defined accountability systems in place, time spent on planning is wasted and children will not be served at an optimal level. *Caution—this is not easy and can be a process that takes years to put in place on district-wide basis.* Some key points about accountability to keep in mind include:
- Accountability starts at the top
- Accountability systems are based upon a crystal-clear definition of success
- The board, the superintendent, and all adults need to accept public and personal responsibility for the success of children
- The outcomes of performance need to be totally transparent

Annual Board Calendar

It is helpful for the board to have an annual calendar for their recurring work. Having such a calendar helps everyone understand what decisions will need to be made in the weeks and months ahead, and help place those decisions in the context of all the other important issues and decisions that they will also need to address. In addition to normal business matters of the district, the board calendar should include annual governance tasks. These would include specific dates/months for:
- The annual organizational meeting

- Quarterly retreats, including formative and summative assessments of governance team and superintendent performance
- Review and reaffirmation of governance team communication and operating protocols
- Reaffirmation of indicators of success and annual targets
- Regular monitoring reports on indicators of success
- Professional development activities of the board
- Community engagement activities
- Dates that they can expect to engage in specific activities, receive specific reports, and work through the budget process
- Activities pertaining to board elections, including candidate orientation, swearing in of new members, and orientation of board members to their new roles and responsibilities

Seeing these tasks laid out for the year can help board members understand the responsibilities that are theirs. Having this board calendar also helps the board feel less dependent upon the superintendent and reduces worry that they may be "missing something" important. **See Appendix G for a very general sample annual calendar of governance activities.** Make sure you add to it, reflecting the context of your system, community, and state.

Board Agenda and Protocols

Nothing can sap board members' energy more than participating in unfocused, rambling, disorganized, or contentious meetings. I've witnessed several examples of poor meeting protocols, including, but not limited to, the following:

> *"All board meetings are part theater."*
> *(Robert Ingram)*

- A board that allowed members to routinely introduce items for action and debate during a board meeting, having no clear process in place for how to get an item on the agenda
- A superintendent who did not draft proposed language for all board actions, then complained about the incomplete or inappropriate actions the board adopted
- A board that allowed unlimited public input on any and all matters and invited public input prior to each and every board action item; their meetings normally ran 6-8 hours in duration

- Boards that engaged in debate with members of the audience during public input sessions
- A board president who allowed speakers during public input time to disrespect district staff members by name
- A superintendent who allowed his executive staff members to sit at the board table and engage in back-and-forth discussion with members during board meetings as though they, too, were members of the board
- A board that met on the stage of a public auditorium, with all board members facing the audience, making it impossible for board members to engage in discussion with each other

I've also witnessed a few great examples of board meeting management:
- One board experiencing severe problems with the public input section of its agenda limited public input to three minutes per speaker and used a timer and a buzzer to strictly administer this guideline
- Another that limited public input at the beginning of the meeting to items on the agenda, limited the number of speakers per issue, and required speakers to sign up in advance; limited time was allowed at the end of the meeting for open public input on general topics related to the district
- One board historically known for its stability met seated at a round table in the center of a large room, so they could better converse with each other—rather than create a show for the audience. They recognized that their meetings were *meetings of the board in public*, rather than *meetings with the public.*
- A board that began every meeting with student recognition or a student performance to remind everyone present why they were there and to set a positive tone for the meeting

There are several simple practices to help with board meeting management. The board should consider adopting these strategies as part of its policies on the conduct of its own work:
- A specific, written process in policy form for development of the board agenda. How do items get on the agenda?
- Specific protocols for staff on preparation of board materials and on presentations to the board
- Pre-meeting information packets that are organized and delivered in a timely fashion (as agreed upon by the governance team)

- Pre-meeting agenda review between superintendent and the board president, and perhaps with all board members at the discretion of the governance team
- Thoughtful arrangement of the board meeting room. Be sure it is set up as a *meeting of the board in public* rather than as a *meeting with the public*. Board members should be able to easily see each other and speak with each other. Executive staff members other than the superintendent are generally not seated at the board table but are readily available at the superintendent's request to present or to respond to questions.
- Adequate staff time dedicated to board meeting planning and anticipation of issues or questions that may arise.
- Start each meeting on time and with a positive note of recognition for staff or students, or with a review of positive things that have happened for kids since the last meeting

> *"Things which matter most must never be at the mercy of things which matter least."*
> *(Goethe)*

- Establish a consent agenda for routine items and personnel appointments, to the extent allowed by state law
- Establish protocols for reasonable public comment, including time limits
- Provide the public in advance with protocols for expected behavior and conduct during board meetings
- The superintendent should include recommended motions for the board's consideration and not leave the clarity of decisions to be made to chance
- Establish protocols for time management of the meetings and control of discussions

One very successful superintendent with whom we have worked presents a "Superintendent's Report" at the beginning of each board meeting. She says it gives her the opportunity to provide information to the board and the public on a variety of topics of interest. Sometimes it may include a controversial issue that she can then frame on her own terms before board members advance their questions. Sometimes it is just routine good news that would otherwise be overlooked. Sometimes it is factual, pertinent and timely information she wants to share. Presenting this report gives her a great platform to frame the messaging on the news of the school district, rather than leaving it to chance.

One peak performing governance team structured their two meetings a month to be different in nature. They hold one monthly voting meeting (preceded by an agenda workshop two days earlier where most of the debate occurs.) Their second meeting of the month is a non-voting workshop that focuses on the system's core business and progress on other indicators of success. So many voting agenda items, by nature, revolve around operational issues and policy, but include little about what is going on in the classroom. The second, non-voting, meeting can also provide opportunities to enhance the board's responsibilities in the area of management oversight. This has been a healthy practice for this particular district.

Special Role of the Board President

The board's bylaws will usually outline the duties of the board president. This is a critical position—a leader among leaders. Under ideal circumstances, the board president will be the superintendent's confidant, liaison, interpreter, caretaker, co-planner, troubleshooter, enforcer, and spokesperson of the board. The position of president requires strength of character, tact, diplomacy, communication and organization skills, plus knowledge of policy, procedure and protocol. Time to do the job well is also a critical asset.

It should almost go without saying that this is **NOT**, as a matter of best practice, a role to be rotated among all board members, with everyone getting a turn. A member should earn this distinction through the quality of their skills and service. If someone is serving the board and the district well in this capacity, do everything you can to keep them in this role. If other board members want this role to serve their own ego needs or political aspirations, try to find other avenues for them to receive public recognition and "air time."

I was fortunate as both a superintendent and as college president to have had high-quality, long-term board chairs. In one case, the chair had served on the board for over 20 years, and as president for more than 10 years. Other members of the board had equally long terms. Unfortunately, over time, as new members came onto the board, some felt they wanted the recognition of the role and the seat began to rotate, not always to the benefit of the organization.

If a superintendent is the beneficiary of a weak or ineffective president, perhaps there is an experienced and respected senior member of the board who can serve as the unofficial "leader among leaders" and unofficial advisor or "coach" to the board president. When neither option is available, the superintendent's role as governance team coach becomes more pronounced and important.

Protocols for Staff Materials

Materials presented to the board in pre-meeting packets or at a meeting should be of a consistent format, style, and quality. Written protocols and standards should be developed for staff preparation of these materials. This is not a time to allow creativity or free-lancing. Board members should know what to expect and where to find it.

For each issue or action item, provide:
- Background and rationale (Why is this issue important? Why are we dealing with it now?)
- Connection to the district indicators of success (How does this matter support our success as a district?)
- Process used and options considered (How did we arrive at this recommendation? What other choices are there and why did we discard them?)
- Findings
- Milestones to come; evaluative measures as we progress
- Recommendations, next steps
- When the board will likely receive more information on this matter, if pertinent

Protocols for Staff Presentations

Staff presentations at board meetings can provide an opportunity for people to shine, or an opportunity for great embarrassment. We've seen superintendents lose favor with their boards because the board did not respect or appreciate key members of the superintendent's leadership team—they often were not prepared to answer questions, fumbled on too long without focus, or weren't properly respectful to board members.

Written protocols should be in place for staff presentations, which would include:
- Following the written summary
- Practicing presentations with other staff
- Time limitations
- A standard format for power point presentations
- Proper salutation of board members
- Proper response to board questions and challenges
- Deferring responses to questions rather than providing inaccurate information to board members

See Appendix H for sample protocols for staff materials and presentations.

Board Committees

John Carver and Don McAdams recommend that there be only one standing board committee—the committee of the whole. They suggest that all board members bear equal responsibility for all areas of their work. Having several subcommittees—the finance committee, the facilities committee, the personnel committee, etc., etc., may seem like a good way to divide up the work, but it has several flaws:
- District staff can get "committee-ed" to death, with preparing for, attending, and doing follow up work for multiple board committees in addition to regular board meetings.
- It provides the opportunity for some board members to be in-the-know and others ignorant on key topics, fueling the opportunity for divisiveness on the board.

> *"Outside of traffic, there is nothing that has held this country back as much as committees."*
> *(Will Rogers)*

- It invites the board to micro-manage day-to-day district operations.
- It allows board members to develop close relationships with key executive staff which has the potential to undermine the superintendent's relationship with the board and puts staff in the position of being directed by individual board members or committees of the board, rather than by the superintendent.

Some boards and superintendents may find it useful to have a two- or three-person Executive Committee of board officers for purposes of agenda development, review and planning the superintendent's evaluation or compensation, or for dealing with other highly sensitive issues. There may also be occasions for short term ad hoc board committees to work on specific policy issues.

I whole-heartedly agree with Carver's and McAdams' perspective on committees of the board.

Governance Team Professional Development Plan

"Best Practice" governance teams understand that they are governing an organization that exists primarily to promote learning. Therefore, they develop an annual plan for the governance team's professional learning and growth. This can range from attending state or national conferences to committing to a regular book study discussion as a group, or to bringing in experts on various aspects of governance during their quarterly retreats. The superintendent can also make a point to regularly include journal articles or other "learning pieces" in weekly board packets.

There is no question that we are at our best when we are growing or helping others grow. Modeling continuous learning at the top of the organization helps to set a tone of commitment to self-initiated, continuous learning for all adults within the school community. It also provides the opportunity for board members to explore ideas and issues outside the context of regularly scheduled meetings, which are all too often laden with public and media angst.

Media Engagement Protocols

One other issue that often creates challenges for superintendents and boards is the entire issue of media engagement and media management. Much has been written on this topic, and there are numerous experts who can work with governance teams on media issues. (This can be a great topic to include in the governance team's professional development plan.)

There are a couple of key areas where problems often arise. The first has to do with the issue of who speaks for the governance team. Obviously, every member of the team has the right to speak to the media on any topic they choose, with the exception of those matters restricted by law. The fact of the matter is, however, that from time to time critical issues arise that call for a more thoughtful and strategic approach with the media. These may include matters that have the potential to trigger law suits, create significant labor problems, or create a public relations disaster for the district. Designating one spokesperson with a well-conceived message, who has the capacity to "stick to the script" with diplomacy and tact, can save a district millions of dollars, not to mention the potential pain and loss of significant public trust. Determining if that person will be the superintendent, the board chair, another board member with significant media experience, or a subject matter expert is a critical first step. Some critical issues may arise where more than one board member feels compelled to speak publicly. In those instances, providing and agreeing upon standard talking points is a next best strategy.

The second area that can create problems (if the superintendent is not sensitive and adept) often arises when a new, bright, and charismatic superintendent is hired. Depending on the district's media market, the new superintendent may become a "media magnet"—the hottest new celebrity in town. In the early going, glowing news stories will be reported and printed reflecting enthusiasm for this fresh face and voice in the community.

This is all understandable to the superintendent's elected bosses for the first few days or even weeks, but if it continues beyond that time frame, there ought to be flashing "caution" lights going off in the superintendent's head. I have observed more than a few superintendents get caught up in the glow of media and community attention, only to turn around and find resentful board members in their shadow. Superintendents need to be mindful that (in most cases) their bosses are the ones who place their names on ballots and run for election every few years. The board members are the ones who need name recognition and whose "political careers" can benefit from positive media and community attention.

Astute superintendents can mitigate this situation by exercising a few simple strategies. Those I've seen be most successful include, but are not limited to, the following suggestions for superintendents:

1. Always, when speaking publicly, recognize and thank any board members present. In their absence, praise the board for the good and hard work they do for kids. Recognize that board work is tough, involves long hours, and is an often thankless job. Make sure they get the public "thanks" at any possible opportunity.
2. When attending events where public and media attention is likely to occur, take a board member or two along (on some agreed upon rotating basis,) and make sure they are introduced and appear in any photo ops that may arise.
3. Over time, when called upon to speak on issues or topics of critical importance to the system, prepare board members to make part or all of the presentation. Do this especially when presentations are made in their own "neck of the woods"—where their constituents and supporters are likely to be present.

This list could go on for pages. The bottom line here is to recognize when it is important for the superintendent to step back and allow the board to shine. After the first few weeks on the job, this should be more often than not.

Attracting and Retaining Quality Board Members

Many superintendents believe that getting involved in board elections is the "kiss of death." I would argue that superintendents can't afford NOT to get involved. They simply need to be thoughtful in proceeding. I offer a few key strategies for attracting quality members, training them, and retaining them, which are summarized below:

- Cultivation of prospective members
- Exit transition protocols
- Board candidate orientation
- New board member orientation
- Swearing-in ceremony

Cultivation of Prospective Members

I have seen few board elections where educational employees and other adult interest groups did not become involved in the recruitment and the campaigns of board candidates. Therefore, the superintendent, other board members, and members of the superintendent's "kitchen cabinet" all have a responsibility to recruit and cultivate high quality board members who will be strong advocates for the interests of children—first and last.

Be intentional and strategic about this. Ideally, the superintendent will not be the one to recruit people to serve, but should make sure someone has assumed responsibility for leading this effort. Every time there is a vacancy on the board, there need to be quality people, with children as a priority, ready to step forward. ***This is too important to leave to chance.***

In cultivating new members, all governance team members should be intentional and mindful of how well your board represents the demographics of your community. Are any key groups not represented? In what areas should potential future members be cultivated?

> *Bad officials are elected by good citizens who do not vote.*
> *(George Jean Nathan)*

In addition to cultivating future members from appropriate demographic groups, potential candidates should be evaluated in the context of their:

- Dedication to the service and interests of all children
- Motivation for serving on the board
- Intellectual capacity and range of experience
- Emotional intelligence
- Time availability and stamina
- Integrity
- Capacity for continuous learning, and, again and most importantly,
- Dedication to the service and interests of all children

Exit Transition Protocols

Some of the more stable and successful boards I've observed have clear understandings and expectations about leaving board service. When possible, ample notice is provided to other members. In fact, some boards have unwritten understandings that members intending to leave board service will resign before their terms are up. This gives the board an opportunity to select a high quality interim member who will then have the opportunity to run as an incumbent. While this may sound a bit Machiavellian, there are few things more important to a school district than having a strong, stable board. Again, ***this is too important to leave to chance.***

Board Candidate Orientation

Don't wait until after the election to have an orientation session. As soon after the filing deadline as possible, the superintendent and board president should host a candidate orientation session. This will help establish a positive relationship with prospective board members. More importantly, it will arm them with facts, hopefully keeping them from making foolish or harmful statements about the district during the course of the election campaign. A final benefit is that is helps them to better understand the commitment they are making. It is a great time to introduce them to the board's position description, communication protocols, standards of practice, and oath of office.

New Member Orientation

On election night, the wise superintendent and board president will call all the candidates, including those who did not win, to congratulate them on either their victory or on a well-run campaign effort and thank them for their interest in the district and its children.

Whenever a new member joins the board, you have a new board. This calls for an orientation retreat with the entire board. This is the opportunity to orient the new members (and re-orient veteran members) about:

- The role and responsibilities of the board. Don't make the mistake of dedicating all of the orientation time to the staff's roles—focus on the job description of the board.
- The district's vision, mission, guiding principles and values, indicators of success, performance targets, and major strategies.
- The district's accountability plan and how it works at every level of the organization
- The board's standards of practice, communication protocols and code of ethics.
- Key board policies and protocols dealing with the board's role and board conduct of business.

I've had the opportunity to work with literally scores of boards whose members have never had the opportunity to be oriented to their roles or responsibilities. They are left guessing as to what they are supposed to do. This is a very poor practice for the governance team of the community's most important organization.

Swearing-in Ceremony

Make the swearing in of new board members a special event. Have them repeat the oath of office. (Videotape it so it can be played it back to them at those times when they may have forgotten what they swore to do.)

Have someone there to take pictures. Invite their families. Celebrate! This is a big deal! They have put themselves and their names out there in the community. And they are about to embark on the most important civic responsibility in your community. This is not the same as joining any other volunteer community board—this is the school board. The future of your community's children is at stake.

In Conclusion

The care and development of boards can be a time consuming challenge for any superintendent. But it is an important and necessary component in building a peak performing governance team.

Adopting the governance team concept, committing to full membership on the team, and assuming ownership for that team's success or failures are major steps toward addressing this challenge.

Then, developing and implementing the policies and protocols that will provide a customized framework of governance for your team to work within can help keep the team focused and on track. We've provided numerous sample documents in the Appendix of this book. *Improve upon all of them as you customize them for use in your district.*

Finally, developing coaching skills can mean the difference between failure at the top of the organization, or a peak performing team leading a powerful system for the benefit of all its children. Coaching 3 to 12 bosses is a role that must be handled with skill and diplomacy. Developing those skills is not something that happens by a one-and-done training session, but, rather, is honed over the course of a career. Boards evolve, as well, so the coaching work is never "done." The superintendent literally needs to become a student of this art.

I hope this book has created an awareness of this new line in the superintendent's position description and some ideas for getting started. Get

> *Do what you can with what you have where you are.*
> *(Theodore Roosevelt)*

moving, if you haven't already done so, and read the Carver and McAdams offerings we suggested earlier, as well as anything else you can find on effective governance teams.

The point is, you're never done learning everything you need to know to handle the challenges of creating and coaching an effective governance team. Transforming a group of individual lay citizens into a peak performing governance team is one of the most important accomplishments a superintendent can pursue—if you want your school system to provide the highest quality education possible for all its children.

APPENDIX

APPENDIX A
What is the Job of the Board?
Sample Board Position Description

The primary purpose of the board is to ensure that the district achieves what it should and that it avoids unacceptable actions and situations. Duties supporting that purpose include:

1. Establish policies in four main areas:
    a. Conduct of board business – how the board carries out its tasks, board member conduct and ethics, effective communications, role of officers, meeting management, board committees, monitoring board performance, etc.
    b. Board-staff relationships – delegation to the superintendent, accountability of the superintendent, and monitoring the performance of the superintendent
    c. Defining district success – clearly specifying what the district is to achieve and clarifying board and staff accountability for that success
    d. Executive limitations – policies that place clear restrictions on the superintendent's and staff's autonomy in pursuing district success

2. Hire a superintendent who will be most able to achieve district success within the limitations established in board policy while maintaining constructive working relationships with those necessary to achieve success; then, adequately and fairly compensate the superintendent and honor all provisions of his or her contract.

3. Establish clear performance expectations for the superintendent and hold the superintendent accountable for day-to-day management of the system and for the system's success.

4. Provide regularly scheduled opportunities for constructive feedback on superintendent performance and on the governance team's performance, with input of the superintendent.

5. Establish and implement an annual plan for monitoring district success and district compliance with its policies; assume public

and personal responsibility for success of the system. Establish a system for ensuring appropriate management oversight of the district.

6. Review and adopt the budget submitted by the superintendent and align resources with district indicators of success.

7. Serve as a connection to the community; promote community understanding and support for the district; help the district remain responsive to community ideas and needs; provide leadership in resolving conflicting community views; build community partnerships and relationships with other community organizations.

8. Help constituents with complaints, problems or issues understand how to obtain resolution by referring them to the appropriate district office.

9. Engage in professional development individually and collectively to improve in effective governance.

10. Serve as advocates for the interests of children before advocating for the interests of any adults.

11. Perform other actions as a full board that may be required by law.

What is the Job of the Superintendent?
Sample Superintendent Position Description

1. Serve as the chief executive officer of the district and as a full, but non-voting, member of the governance team.

2. Assume administrative responsibility, accountability and leadership for achieving the district's indicators of success as adopted by the board.

3. Manage the day-to-day operations of the district within the policy parameters as adopted by the board, assuming responsibility and authority for the planning, operation, supervision, assignment, and evaluation of the programs, services, staff, students and facilities of the district.

4. Prepare recommendations for policies to be adopted by the Board; undertake the implementation of adopted policies; develop appropriate administrative procedures to implement policies adopted by the Board.

5. Prepare and submit to the Board a proposed annual budget reflecting district priorities as identified in the district's strategic plan and aligned with district indicators of success.

6. Provide the Board with accurate and timely information that enables the Board to appropriately perform its monitoring function.

7. Make recommendations regarding selection or termination of the district's staff, consistent with laws of the State and district policy.

8. Communicate and collaborate with all members of the Board, keeping the Board up-to-date on developments, initiatives and issues in the district; provide leadership to enable the Board to function effectively.

9. Act as liaison between the district and the community, assuming responsibility for effective public relations and for creating a

cooperative working relationship between the schools and the community.

10. Assume the role of the district's first learner, first teacher, first advocate, and first collaborator on behalf of children.

11. Stay abreast of educational trends and developments by participating in appropriate professional development.

12. Perform all other duties of the office of Superintendent as may be prescribed by law.

APPENDIX B

The Superintendent's Contract
Sample Language

Sample #1: No Meddling Clause

The Board, individually and collectively, shall promptly refer all criticisms, complaints and suggestions called to its/their attention to the Superintendent for study and recommendation, and shall refrain from individual interference with the administration of school policies, except through Board action.

Sample #2: No Meddling Clause

The Superintendent shall be the chief executive officer of the district and shall have all of the powers and rights necessary to carry out that role. Although the governing board retains ultimate power and authority over decisions affecting the district, the governing board shall not unreasonably interfere with the day-to-day decision-making processes of the Superintendent. The governing board retains the right to question, approve, or disapprove in its discretion as it deems appropriate the decisions that Superintendent makes, but shall not insert itself into the day-to-day deliberative processes in which Superintendent engages.

Sample #3: Consequences for Violation of Contract

The Superintendent may elect to terminate his Employment Contract for Good Reason with 90-day's notice during the term of the Employment Contract and be delivered in writing to each member of the governing board. "Good Reason" is defined as:
> a. Any failure by the governing board to comply with any material provision of this Employment Contract which has not been cured within 30 days after written notice of such noncompliance has been given by Superintendent to the President of the governing board;
> c. In the reasonable discretion of the Superintendent, any single member or combination of members of the governing board unreasonably interfere(s) with the day-to-day administration of the district.

In the event the Superintendent exercises this option, the Superintendent agrees to relinquish any claims which he may have against the district in return for the payment specified in this paragraph. In acknowledgement of the difficulty or impossibility of calculating possible damages to the Superintendent as a result of such termination, the cash settlement amount of liquidated damages shall be an amount equal to the monthly salary of the Superintendent multiplied by the number of months remaining on his Employment Contract, but not to exceed six months.

APPENDIX C
Model Standards of Practice
Governance Team

As elected members of the board of the _____ Public Schools, we accept the high honor and trust that has been placed in us to ensure that the children of this district receive the best education available anywhere in the United States of America. In accepting this role, we hold the pursuit of that goal as our sacred duty. To that end, we hereby commit to the following in the conduct of our business. We will:

- Place the interests of children above all others in every decision that we make;
- Uphold all applicable federal and state laws and regulations;
- Abide by the policies of the Board, and work with fellow governance team members to change those policies as needed to improve student learning;
- Maintain board focus on the achievement of all students regardless of race, class, ethnicity, or gender;
- Not use our positions for personal or partisan gain;
- Model continuous learning in our roles as members of the governance team;
- Maintain a strategic plan for the district that clearly defines success and accountability for the board, the staff, and our students;
- Focus on the policy work of the Board and monitor progress on the indicators of success in our strategic plan, leaving the day to day operation of the district to the superintendent and staff;
- Base our decisions upon available facts, vote our convictions, avoid bias, and uphold and support the decisions of the majority of the board once a decision is made;
- Work to build trust between and among board members and the superintendent by treating everyone with dignity and respect, even in times of disagreement;
- Maintain the confidentiality of privileged information including that shared in executive sessions of the board;
- Recognize that authority rests only with majority decisions of the board and will make no independent commitments or take any independent actions that may compromise the board as a whole;

- Refer constituent complaints and concerns to the appropriate person within the district chain of command; and
- Respect the leadership roles of the board chair and superintendent.

We will maintain fidelity to these commitments and will be held accountable by our fellow board members should any one of us fail to live up to these commitments.

Signed:

_____

_____

_____

_____

_____

_____

_____

_____

APPENDIX D
Model Oath of Office
Board of Education

As an elected member of the board of the _____ Public Schools, I accept the high honor and trust that has been placed in me to ensure that the children of this district receive the best education available anywhere in the United States of America. In accepting this position, I hold the pursuit of that goal as my sacred duty. To that end, I hereby swear that I will:

- Place the interests of children above all others in every decision that I make;
- Uphold all applicable federal and state laws and regulations;
- Abide by the policies of the Board, and work with my fellow Board members to change those policies as needed to improve student learning;
- Maintain board focus on the achievement of all students regardless of race, class, ethnicity, or gender;
- Not use my position for personal or partisan gain;
- Model continuous learning in my role as a member of the governance team;
- Maintain a strategic plan for the district that clearly defines success and accountability for the board, the staff, and our students;
- Focus on the policy work of the Board and monitor progress on the indicators of success in our strategic plan, leaving the day to day operation of the district to the superintendent and staff;
- Base my decisions upon available facts, vote my convictions, avoid bias, and uphold and support the decisions of the majority of the board once a decision is made;
- Work to build trust between and among board members and the superintendent by treating everyone with dignity and respect, even in times of disagreement;
- Maintain the confidentiality of privileged information including that shared in executive sessions of the board;
- Recognize that authority rests only with majority decisions of the board and will make no independent commitments or take any independent actions that may compromise the board as a whole;

- Refer constituent complaints and concerns to the appropriate person within the district chain of command; and
- Respect the leadership roles of the board chair and superintendent.

I will maintain fidelity to these commitments and will be held accountable by my fellow board members should I fail to live up to this oath. So help me, God.

This oath of office has been sworn to on this, the _____ day of _____, 20__.

_____   _____
Trustee   Witness

APPENDIX E
Model Protocols for
Board Superintendent Communication

1. We recognize that the superintendent is the only employee of the district who reports to seven bosses, therefore communication protocols are not only necessary, but must be established in order to maintain effective communications between the superintendent, board, and all constituent groups of the system.

2. As superintendent, you can expect me to keep you as fully informed as needed to effectively fulfill your responsibilities.

3. This communication will be provided through my office via the following methods:
   a. Monthly board meetings and board study sessions
   b. Quarterly governance team retreats
   c. Quarterly superintendent/board member one-on-one interviews
   d. Weekly written updates
   e. Periodic phone check-ins
   f. Periodic one-on-one face-to-face meetings as necessary
   g. Urgent calls or emails to alert you to events you're likely to hear about through the media or from your neighbors
   h. Information requested by any member will be distributed to all members
   i. If I have a concern about something you have done or have not done, you will hear it from me only.
   j. Media advisories and press releases
   k. Planning meetings with the board president/vice president

4. As superintendent, I need the following from you if I am going to do my job effectively:
   a. Be a good listener to constituent concerns
   b. Refer employee concerns to the point of the problem and/or to their union representative if a contract violation is alleged. Inform me so that I can ensure the issue is handled properly.

c. Refer constituent concerns or complaints to the point of the problem, and, through the appropriate chain of command, to my office if necessary.

d. If you believe that a concern raised by a constituent is of a potentially serious nature or may require a board policy change, inform me immediately.

e. If you need information on any aspect of the district, please communicate this request to my office so that I can ensure that your needs are met.

f. Remember that as a board member, your electronic communications are public information.

g. If you have a concern about something that I have done or have not done, reciprocate the courtesy outlined in 3.i.

h. Maintain fidelity to your fellow board members, your board policies and governance team standards when communicating with the media.

APPENDIX F

Sample Board Policy:
Board Member Violation of Policy

The governance team has established a clear understanding of mutual commitments in the conduct of governance team business, standards of practice and communication protocols. All governance team members, including the superintendent, are expected to abide by these policies as well as maintain a fidelity to all other district board policies.

_____ (board designee) shall have the responsibility of enforcing said policies. In the event that a governance team member violates any of the above commitments, the following actions shall be taken.

I. First Offense

The board designee shall meet with the individual to explain the offense and to secure a commitment that it will not reoccur in the future.

II. Second Offense

The board designee may choose, depending upon the seriousness of the offense and the amount of time since the prior offense, to:
   a) meet with the individual to explain the offense and secure a commitment that it will not reoccur in the future
   b) issue a verbal notice of policy violation
   c) issue a written notice of policy violation with copies sent to all members of the governance team, or
   d) issue a written notice of policy violation, read the notice at the next public meeting of the board, and request board action to sanction the board member in violation

II. Further Offenses

Further offenses shall be dealt with by the board designee in the same manner as outlined above. Depending upon the seriousness and/or frequency of the offenses, the board designee may further propose for board action:
   a) a public request for the offending member's resignation from the board, or

b) the initiation by the board of a campaign to have the offending board member recalled from office by a vote of the people.

APPENDIX G
Sample Annual Calendar for Effective Governance

The following items or actions are those that the board is responsible for addressing on an annual basis; ordinarily they occur in the months shown below, although this will vary by district. These governance items are in addition to other policy issues the board must act on throughout the year.

Month	Action Item
July	Annual organizational meeting • Reaffirm board standards of practice and communication protocols • Reaffirm district indicators of success and targets • New board member induction and oath of office • Election and induction of officers • Adoption of retreat schedule for the year
August	Progress report on indicator(s) of success Management oversight report(s) to board
September	Quarterly retreat • Formative performance assessment of the superintendent • Reaffirm superintendent's position description, assessment process, professional development plan • Discussion of governance team performance, assessment process, professional development plan • Board professional development
October	Progress report on indicator(s) of success Management oversight report(s) to board
November	Progress report on indicator(s) of success Management oversight report(s) to board
December	Quarterly retreat • Formative performance assessment of the superintendent • Discussion of board performance • Board professional development
January	Progress report on indicator(s) of success Management oversight report(s) to board
February	Progress report on indicator(s) of success

	Management oversight report(s) to board
March	Quarterly retreat • Summative performance assessment of the superintendent • Discussion of board performance • Act on superintendent contract/compensation
April	Progress report on indicator(s) of success Management oversight report(s) to board
May	Progress report on indicator(s) of success Management oversight report(s) to board
June	Quarterly retreat • Formative performance assessment of the superintendent • Discussion of board performance • Board professional development

APPENDIX H

Sample Protocols for Staff Preparation of Board Meeting Materials

1. Potential board agenda items submitted by staff are to be presented to the superintendent a minimum of two weeks prior to said meeting, with few exceptions.

2. Staff-prepared materials for the board are to be submitted to the superintendent no less than one week prior to a board meeting.

3. For any report to the board generated by staff, staff committee, task force or vendor, the submitting administrator will provide an executive summary of no more than three pages. The executive summary should be printed on 8-1/2 x 11" white paper in 14 point font and include the following:
   a. Cover including
      i. Appropriate title of topic
      ii. Date
      iii. Name of administrator
      iv. Notation indicating "for information only" or "action required"
   b. Those responsible for developing the report and those who contributed to the report generation.
   c. Issue background and rationale for consideration
   d. How this issue supports or addresses district goals and strategies
   e. Methodology or process utilized to reach this point in decision-making; major tasks completed or underway
   f. Key issues and options considered, including advantages and disadvantages of each
   g. Findings
   h. Major milestones ahead
   i. Evaluation measures
   j. Recommendations, if any

Sample Protocols for
Staff Presentations to the Board

1. Staff presentations to board will generally follow the outline of the written executive summary.

2. Presentations will be made to the superintendent and executive staff one week prior to the board meeting for practice and feedback.

3. Staff members should anticipate and address board questions in the text of the report.

4. Presentations will, with rare exception, be of no more than ten minutes in duration, plus time for board Q & A.

5. Presentations will be made from a designated standing position.

6. Presentations may be supported by power point or other visuals.
    a. Presentations should include no more than 5-7 slides, with 3-5 bullets per page.
    b. Bullets should include no more than 5-7 words. Use the bullets to pull the audience through the presentation as a visual reference; do not read from bullets word-for-word or use the bullets as a script.
    c. Use the standard district template, including standard fonts, design and colors. Do not add clip art. Do not add photos unless critical to the presentation and of excellent quality.
    d. Make sure tables and graphs are legible to an audience member sitting in the back of the room.
    e. Proofread carefully, and never serve as the lone proofreader.
    f. Practice key presentations in advance. Anticipate questions, and have answers prepared in advance. Recognize when questions are really speeches, and do not respond.

7. Presenters will address board members as Mr., Mrs., Ms., Dr., or other appropriate salutation.

8. Staff should never display disrespect or anger in response to board questions, actions, or reactions.

(Major source: Nora Carr, former Chief Communications Officer, Charlotte-Mecklenburg Schools)

APPENDIX I

Sample Governance Team Assessment Tool

Rating Scale: *5 = Area of Strength*
4 = Area Showing Promise or Progress
3 = Neither an Area of Strength or a Problem Area
2 = Area Needs Some Additional Focus
1 = A Problem Area

	5	4	3	2	1
Peak Performing Governance Team Basics					
Team members are united by their commitment to the service of children.					
The board and superintendent have an interdependent relationship.					
Indicators of success are established for the district.					
Governance team relationships are based upon trust and respect.					
The governance team has developed strong and durable linkages with the community.					
Foundational Elements					
A position description for the board has been established and adopted as policy.					
A position description for the superintendent has been established and adopted as policy.					
The superintendent's contract appropriately clarifies the respective roles of the superintendent and the board.					
Criteria, process, and time line for superintendent's performance evaluation are clearly stated in superintendent's contract and/or in adopted board policy.					
Criteria, process, and time line for board's performance evaluation have been adopted; board assessment occurs along with the superintendent's evaluation.					
A quarterly calendar for board retreats has been established, which include formative input on board/superintendent performance.					

	5	4	3	2	1
Governance team standards of practice and oath of office are in place, clearly articulating parameters for the conduct of governance team business and acceptable board behavior.					
Communication protocols for board and superintendent have been clearly articulated.					
Responsibility has been assigned for enforcement of board standards of practice, oath of office and board policy; consequences for violation are clear and reviewed by the board on an annual basis.					
Superintendent has established and utilizes a "kitchen cabinet" as needed.					
Governance Team in Action					
A dynamic plan and planning process have been adopted by the board, clearly defining district success and district-wide responsibility for success.					
The board as a whole has assumed public and personal accountability for district success.					
The board holds the superintendent publicly and personally accountable for implementing the plan and moving the district towards success as defined. An accountability system has been established for all district staff.					
An annual board action and retreat calendar has been established to ensure and protect the time board members will need to conduct their business.					
Protocols for agenda planning, review, and format have been established and adopted by the board.					
The role of the board president has been established.					
Protocols for staff preparation of board materials have been established and are enforced.					
Protocols for staff presentations to the board have been established and are enforced.					
The board generally operates as a committee of the whole, with standing and ad hoc committees kept to a minimum.					

	5	4	3	2	1
An annual plan for board professional development has been established.					
Protocols for media engagement have been established.					
Attracting and Retaining Quality Board Members					
A board committee or the "kitchen cabinet" has been charged with identifying and cultivating prospective board members who reflect the needs of the community.					
Conversation is held with board members about exit transition protocols in order to sustain stability on the board.					
When openings for appointment or election occur, the superintendent and board chair conduct an orientation session for all candidates.					
Following the election of new members, a board member orientation session is held, covering the role of the governing board.					
An official, formal swearing-in ceremony for new board members is conducted that includes a substantive oath of office.					
Adherence to Standards of Practice *All Members of the Governance Team:*					
Place the interests of children above all others in every decision made.					
Uphold all applicable federal state laws and regulations.					
Abide by board policies and work with fellow team members to change policies as need to improve student learning.					
Maintain focus on the achievement of all students regardless of race, class, ethnicity, or gender.					
Do not use board positions for personal or partisan gain.					
Model continuous learning in their roles as governance					

	5	4	3	2	1
team members.					
Maintain a strategic plan that clearly defines success and accountability.					
Focus on the policy work of the board, leaving day-to-day operations to the staff.					
Base decisions upon facts, avoid bias, and support decisions of the board once decisions are made.					
Work to build trust between and among board members by treating everyone with dignity and respect, even in times of disagreement.					
Maintain the confidentiality of privileged information.					
Recognize that authority rests with majority decisions of the board and make no independent commitments or actions that compromise the board as a whole.					
Refer constituent concerns to the appropriate person within the district.					
Respect the leadership roles of the board chair and superintendent.					

About the Authors

Timothy G. Quinn

Dr. Timothy G. Quinn's career spans teaching and leadership at all levels of public education from K-12 through community college and university. He served as an English teacher, assistant principal, and principal in Michigan, prior to becoming superintendent of the Green Bay Public Schools and serving a term as Wisconsin's Deputy State Superintendent of Instruction. He also served as president of Northwestern Michigan College in Traverse City, Michigan. Dr. Quinn was then appointed by The University of Michigan as chief executive officer of Michigan's first virtual college.

Dr. Quinn was the founder and former president of the highly successful Michigan Leadership Institute, which is dedicated to leadership development, placement of outstanding leaders, and continuous research on the topic of leadership. As a result of the Institute's work, Tim was engaged by The Eli and Edythe Broad Foundation to partner on the creation of The Broad Center for the Management of School Systems and the Broad Superintendents Academy.

In these roles, Dr. Quinn has worked with hundreds of governing boards and superintendents around the country, in urban, suburban and rural districts of all sizes, as well as with boards of charter school organizations. He has facilitated board retreats and board training sessions, conducted governance team performance assessments, and has trained and coached superintendents on how to create an effective board/superintendent partnership. In addition, Tim has served on the boards of several human services and not-for-profit organizations.

Tim earned a Ph.D. in educational leadership from The University of Michigan, and received honorary doctoral degrees for his statewide leadership from Eastern Michigan, Central Michigan and Grand Valley State Universities.

Michelle (Shelley) Keith

Michelle E. Keith's career includes twenty years of higher education experience in the areas of human resources, planning and governance. As a human resources administrator at Iowa State University and as the Director of Human Resources at Northwestern Michigan College, she has had extensive experience in recruitment, employment, and professional development.

Shelley was the co-founder and former vice president of the Michigan Leadership Institute, and was engaged by The Eli and Edythe Broad Foundation to partner on the creation and management of the Broad Superintendents Academy.

She has a bachelor's degree and master's degree from Iowa State University.

CPSIA information can be obtained at www.ICGtesting.com
Printed in the USA
LVOW05s2254020314

375616LV00010B/346/P